# EVERYONE IS AN EXPERT
## (about something)

## The Search for Meaning Online

### By Seth Godin

**EVERYONE'S AN EXPERT (ON SOMETHING) Seth Godin**

*THIS BOOK is for anyone who wants more online traffic, more revenue, more followers, more attention, more interest, more donations or more influence.*
*The paradox, of course, is that the best way to get all these things is by delivering less.*
*This is a book about focus and meaning. Feel free to share it.*

# Table of Contents

NOTE! This is almost the sequel to my ebook *Who's There?*

which was a short riff about blogging.

*Everyone's an Expert* is designed for people who are already familiar with the idea of blogs (hey, you might even *have* a blog) and AdWords and RSS and other Web 2.0 goodies. If you'd like to start by reading the slightly less-techy intro version, read online *Who's There* at: *http://sethgodin.typepad.com/seths_blog/2005/09/ whos_there_the_.html*.

Thanks for reading. When you're done, feel free to post this on your blog or email it to whomever you believe would benefit.


AN EXPERIMENT: A big experiment. It's an exercise in amplifying the voices of people with something to say, at the same time that we build a community, a site that's free to use, a co-op that pays

royalties to its members, *and* a way to raise millions of dollars for charity—from New Orleans to Tanzania.

This is an ebook about a brand new online company and, more important, about a new sort of online tool that might very well change the way you discover (and publish) information.

For most of us, it's not about the money at all—it's about spreading our ideas.

# FOUR QUESTIONS

How do I get more traffic to my site?
How do I find what I'm looking for on the web?
Where are the experts?
Can I be one?

LET'S SAY YOU JUST DISCOVERED ESPRESSO. For years and years, you were afraid to try it,
sticking with herbal tea and the like, but one day, wrestling with boredom and hunger at
O'Hare, you broke down and ordered a decaf latte at Starbucks. And fell in love.

Now, you *love* espresso. You need it. All the time. But you really don't want to spend your entire income at Starbucks, and you believe, deep down, that maybe it's possible to make even better espresso at home.

So, you do the obvious thing. You go to Google. And you type in "buy espresso machine."

Of course, you're not ready to buy an espresso machine right this second. Even if the perfect machine at the perfect price from the right vendor appeared in a Google ad at the top of your screen, there's no way on earth you'd buy that machine right now. Right now, you're *just looking*. You just want to learn about what's going on.

So, you do your search and find way more than 820,000 matches. The first few are triumphs of Search Engine Optimization (SEO). These sites sell espresso machines and have done a great job of getting listed high up in the Google results. But that, of course, is not what you want. You don't want to only see the listings of machines, not yet. You want to understand what's important, what matters, what's worth it. Seeing the machines now is like
shopping for a car before you know how to drive. Without meaning, it's a waste of time.

A few sites down the list, I found that Engadget.com, a site I know and trust, has an article. So you click on it.

It's a pretty worthless article. But you notice that there are literally hundreds of comments. You click and read a few.

The first few comments are worthless because they are unsubstantiated boasts from people you've never heard of. But about five comments down, you discover a long, thoughtful post by someone who knows all about espresso machines. Not everyone is seduced by rational textual argument, but you are, so you get excited. Finally! You're starting to understand.

So you go to www.coffeegeek.com , which you find through another comment. Nirvana! This is the site that should have been #1. But alas, it's disorganized and hard to follow. So you spend three hours (I'm not kidding, three hours) reading up on espresso. Now you're informed, you know what's out there and you've read a few reviews of different machines. Finally, you know enough to think about buying.

So you go back to your original Google search. And now you click on an ad. You look at that site for a while, hit Back, click on another ad. After you've clicked on six ads, you decide to go back to coffeegeek and buy a $1,400 espresso machine.

Did you know that those ads sell for about $5.50 a click?

You clicked on six of them. That's $33 Google earned because of your incessant clicking. And you ended up buying somewhere else. Google deserves every penny, of course, because even though you didn't buy anything, you were exactly the kind of prospect the advertisers were looking for. You just weren't ready yet. This is the best advertising the Web has to offer.

Congratulations. Now you understand how surfing the Web really works. You used to think that a magic search engine would find your answer and you'd be done.
Not so. You found clues, you invested time, and you turned it into meaning.
Since 1994, Web 1.0 has been an ongoing effort to give you more (and better) clues. Web 2.0 is about something else entirely.

# This book has a pretty simple thesis

I BELIEVE THAT WHEN YOU GO ONLINE, you don't *search*. You don't even *find*. Instead, you are usually on a quest to *make sense*. That's the goal of most visits to Google or Yahoo! or blogs or the Wikipedia. How do you make sense of the noise that's coming at you from all directions?

You won't take action—you won't buy something, book something, hire someone, or take a position on a political issue—until you've made sense of your options.

Think about the way you shop—online or in the real world. Unless the item is a staple or the store is quite familiar, it's unlikely that you buy the very first option you come across. Instead, you circle the store, putting off the salespeople ("I'm just browsing"), or you click around the Web, poking and exploring and searching until you understand your options. You're not seeking the answer at first —first you want to understand the meaning behind your choices.

Before you download that software or buy that product, you might want a better understanding of how a technology works. Or you might want to find three or four choices for your budget before you book your hotel in London. You might want to be more comfortable about the ways to persuade your school board not to ban a certain book, or you

11

might want to know how Moby's new album is coming along.

If this sounds a little like word of mouth, that should come as no surprise. Not only does word of mouth give us confidence in a decision, it acts as a filter. It gets rid of the extraneous and presents just the focused good stuff.

Sooner or later, you'll figure out whatever it is you're trying to understand. Sooner or later, the picture will snap into focus, and then you'll stop investing your time on *researching* the issue and take *action* instead. After that, maybe you'll take your newfound understanding and use it to teach and persuade others (after all, now you're an expert). Or maybe you'll move on to discover something else.

Searching online should really be called *poking* online. Because that's what you do. You poke around. You poke in Google or at Yahoo! and you poke at some ads. You're not ready to take action, but you are willing to spend a few minutes poking.

After looking at a bunch of links and pages, then, *finally*, you get it. You understand enough to take action—to buy something or make a decision. The thing is, this takes a long time. The Web ought to accelerate and even replicate that word of mouth phenomenon that works so well in the real world.

The mistake: The engineers who built the Web believed that if they presented the "right" answer, intelligent humans would be pleased. In fact, before you get it, before you discover the meaning, **there is no right answer.**

# EVERYONE'S AN EXPERT (ON SOMETHING) Seth Godin

# The first version of the Web was about using computers to assemble clues

IF YOU GO TO GOOGLE today and type in "seth", it will present you with millions of "clues" as to who you might mean. As I write this, more than 28 million pages are returned by Google's vast index, and the right answer is in there somewhere.

The powerful Google algorithm, combined with the nearly instantaneous Google servers, put that information together in a heartbeat. And now it's up to you to figure out the clues, to find the right page and be happy.

You *could* click on a few of the links on the first page of matches. You *could* click on some AdWords. Or you could reject Google's hierarchy of pages and jump to page 32 of the countless pages of matches to see what's there. You could click on one of the matches, sniff that page, and perhaps click on some of the links on that page, and so on, for a long, long time.

It's a lot of information and a lot of work. You don't even realize that you perform this poking ritual almost every time you search, but you do. Yet most of us don't have the time and energy to do the detective work for more than a minute or two, which is why most Web searches fail. Over time, users are realizing that their searches are not reaching their expectations, which is why the quest for a better way to search continues. Google built a better clue machine and we raced to use it.

If clues are what you need, then more is the answer. More clues, more links, more sites.

But what if there were a librarian you trusted? What if she had a desk near yours, or she was available on some instant messaging program, a click away, standing by, waiting to hear from you? You could say, "Hey Sarah, there's a reference on Scoble's blog to a guy named Seth. Who's that?" And she would know. And she could tell you in two or three sentences, and the picture would snap into place and you could go back to work. Because Sarah is trusted, and because she's a person—a person who understands ideas and context and relevance, she could give you meaning far faster and with far more authority than a computer ever could.

The first version of the Web—the clue machine—continues to get better and faster and more complete. The first version of the Web is, in essence, a miracle, something few people could have predicted even ten years ago.

But the first version of the Web is still focused on poking. It always will be. *It delivers matches, but it doesn't deliver meaning.*

# EVERYONE'S AN EXPERT (ON SOMETHING) Seth Godin

# The second version of the Web is about enabling people to share meaning

IF YOU WANT TO KNOW how much tickets to *The Odd Couple* on Broadway are really worth, a quick search on eBay will let you know. You'll find dozens of sellers and hundreds of bidders, all working in a transparent way to determine the value of an item.

If you want to know one person's perspective on the latest Washington scandal, that's pretty easy to discover as well. Go visit her blog, and you can read all about it. You can read what she's saying today, and with a little scrolling, compare it to what she said yesterday or last week. You can also read the TrackBacks and the comments and see what others are saying about her posts.

There are two things going on here:

The first is that people like to *listen.* They like to listen to people they agree with and to people they trust. They go online to hear what others have to say. You do this every day. So do I.

And the second is that people like to *talk.* This, of course, is no surprise to you, but it appears to have stumped the first generation of media conglomerates that have tried to control the conversation online.

17

People like to talk about what's on their minds. People like to talk about the products they use. They like to talk about the music on their iPods and the hotel they loved in Paris. They like to talk about celebrities and calamities and science and math and even brands of sneakers. It's not trivia if it means something to you.

That's why there are 80,000 new blogs *every single day*. That's more blogs started every *day* than there are books published every year in the United States.

Everybody is an expert about something.

Everybody has a passion, a hobby and a cause. And you're justifiably proud of your point of view.

We—all of us—want to share our expertise, to discover what people think about our point of view. But if you share it all, all at once, no one will find you. We all must *focus* our expertise. We need to refine it and make it more useful—to us and to the world.

A blog is a great first step. But this is about something that makes your blog work better.

# Blogs are time-based, like movies

THE BEST BLOGS HAVE A REGULAR READERSHIP.

Because so many blog readers are regulars, returning every day or every week, the blogger has the luxury of using just a few words to pick up where she left off. She can invent conventions, pursue open topics, pick up dropped threads, and talk in a vernacular that her readers enjoy.

When I post to my blog (http://sethgodin.typepad.com/), I know that the vast majority of my readers read what I wrote last week and last month as well. That makes it easier for me to make a point without a lot of backtracking.

A great blog is an ongoing exposition of meaning on the blogger's chosen topic(s) within a particular point of view. A great blog is like a movie, in that seeing one frame doesn't help you an awful lot. Sure, if you're lucky, the one frame you see will be Neo and Morpheus in the middle of a kung fu fight. But with your luck, it will just as likely be a frame of gibberish on a cool black background. Movies work because directors know that people are watching *the whole thing*, not just a frame. The same thing is true of blogs.

Here's a blog post in its entirety: "Yesterday, I was wrong. So was Doc."

This is meaningless if you haven't been reading all along. Regular readers get it instantly, of course.

But what if you, the online listener, the person in search of meaning, don't have the patience or the time for a long-term commitment? What if you need meaning *right now* so you can get on with the next thing on your agenda?

Blogs are deep and dense and gradual and effective. Blogs can change minds over time. By combining the permission marketing (http://www.amazon.com/exec/obidos/ASIN/068485 6360/permissionmarket/103-9124595-5211034) aspects of RSS (http://sethgodin.typepad.com/seths_blog/2005/08/ whats_rss.html) and subscription with the credibility the author gets as he speaks powerfully, a blog can have a large impact on people.

But sometimes you want people to *leave*. Leave and go to another site you recommend. Leave and buy something you raved about. Leave and listen to a song or look at a few pictures.

Some days my blog features a relatively profound post. Other days, it leads with a silly commentary or some dufus picture. The timing of your first visit has a lot to do with what you will think of me for a long, long time. Come on a good day and you'll think I'm smart. Come on a bad day and your first impression will forever be that I'm sort of goofy.

It's a little like basing the Academy Awards on the opinions of judges who have only seen one randomly selected frame of your movie.

Must I have a blog that's useful only for regular readers? How can I answer the question "What do I do now?" when it's asked by someone who has never visited my blog before? How can I share my experience and my knowledge in a faster and more direct way?

**EVERYONE'S AN EXPERT (ON SOMETHING)** Seth Godin

# Sometimes we need a starting point, not a movie. We need a nowblog

TELL ME WHAT I NEED TO KNOW RIGHT NOW.

Point me in the right direction.

Put all the clues on the table at once. Tell me at a glance whether I can trust you and how I can discover the meaning I seek.

That's what most Web surfers want. That's what *everyone* often wants.

And that's been missing from the Web.

We need a nowblog. A place where a stranger can go to get insight and meaning—and then leave that site and go somewhere else. Leave to go back to work, or leave to read your best blog posts, or leave to go transact somewhere else online.

A nowblog is a place, the best place to start. I call this place a **lens**.

So, here's the deal: I want you to go build some lenses.

**EVERYONE'S AN EXPERT (ON SOMETHING) Seth Godin**

# Introducing lenses

A LENS FILTERS LIGHT AND SHOWS US WHAT WE NEED TO SEE. It focuses on some elements and hides others.
Lenses are often different and frequently personal. ("Don't wear your friend's glasses," mom shouts; "you might go blind!")

An online lens is a page, a *single page*, that highlights one person's view of the Web—not the whole Web, just one tiny part of it.

A lens gives context. When it succeeds, it delivers meaning.

A lens can tell you which books, records, and Web sites are the best way to appreciate Miles Davis. A lens can show you the ten most important things you need to know about copyright on the Web. A lens can highlight the key players in the hospital crib business and give you the confidence you need to go ahead and buy something—
without worrying about whether you missed a key player or didn't understand a critical choice.

A lens quickly answers the question "What do I need to know?"

I call the person who makes a lens a *lensmaster*. A lensmaster uses the tools available online to

provide links, feeds, abstracts, and lists to users who are trying to make sense of a topic. These are users in search of meaning, users in
a hurry, users who won't wait.

Give users meaning, and they are far more likely to take action.

# Lenses are personal

LIKE MOST EBAY SELLERS OR VIRTUALLY ALL SUCCESSFUL BLOGGERS, lensmasters are individuals with strong personal agendas, expertise, causes, products and even opinions. They are not employed or directed by a corporation. Lensmasters build their lenses for fun, or for ego, or to drive traffic to their corporate sites or their blogs. Lensmasters build lenses to raise money for charity or to earn royalty checks for themselves.

Blogs were a breakthrough because they allowed intensely personal thoughts to be shared (over time) online. A lens is the perfect companion to a blog. A lens amplifies a blog; it doesn't replace it. A lens gives the surfer a window into a blog and into the world that surrounds it.

A lens doesn't pretend to deliver the complete truth, any more than a blog does. Instead, a lens says, "Here's my take on what you need to know about this topic." The topic might be your favorite business books, or everything you know about bars in San Diego, or lists of reasons to support your local alderman. The topic might be the lensmaster himself! Where better for people to find out about you than on a page you build? A page that points to your résumé and your photos and your Flickr account and your current employer. *If you don't claim your name, who will?*

The idea is simple: A lens provides meaning and the links necessary to take action on that meaning. A lens is a guide. Provide the meaning, and the surfer will go ahead and take the action.

# Lenses are connected

UNLIKE A BLOG, just about every single item in a lens is connected to something on the Web. Lenses don't *hold* content. They *point* to content. And like all good guides, they comment on what they point to.

So your lens can point to blogs or to predefined Yahoo! searches or to a MapQuest map to your favorite restaurant. Your lens can point to the weather report or to treasured books on Amazon or to your wedding pictures on Flickr. A lens isn't filled with content. It points to content.

And your lens also points to other lenses. Lenses on similar topics. Lenses by people you know and trust. Lenses that are highly rated by Web surfers, and lenses that a lot of other people have linked to.

A lens doesn't work unless a Web surfer can find it when she needs it. And a lens doesn't work unless it's easy to build and and even easier to maintain.

That's why we're launching a co-op called
**Squidoo.com.**

Squidoo lets lensmasters build lenses quickly.
Then it connects those lenses to other relevant
lenses and provides a search engine to make it
easy for any Web surfer to find the right lens at
the right time.

# Make it pay

THE BENEFITS OF A LENS include:
- Lenses are free.
- . A royalty payment. Royalties are earned from all the keyword clicks, affiliate income, and referral fees the lenses generate.
- More traffic to your blog and your Web sites.
- A way to build credibility for yourself and your organization by serving as a trusted guide.
- Increased search engine rank for you and the pages you point to.

Lenses are free. You can start one at no cost, Squidoo will host it for you at no cost, and you can even generate a profit. Your royalty payments can be sent directly to you or to your favorite charity or organization. Our goal as a co-op is to pay as much money as we can to charities and to lensmasters.

**EVERYONE'S AN EXPERT (ON SOMETHING) Seth Godin**

# Build your own

MAKE NO MISTAKE. You can build your own lens, right now. You don't need help from me or from Squidoo. You don't need permission from anyone. You can hire a designer, get some hosting, and build a page. That page can have ads from Google or Yahoo! or someone else, so you can make money if you need to pay the overhead. Your page can have links to sites you like. It can aggregate RSS feeds or feature searches you've done on your cosen topic.

Once you build a lens, you can compute how much you're making on the average visitor. Or you can discover how good a job you're doing in teaching people what you were hoping to teach them. And once you discover that, you can invest money in buying AdWord traffic or doing other sorts of promotions to get visitors to your lens.

There are lenses all over the Web. They're not very well organized, though. And they are hard to find and they're not very well linked. And they cost too much to build. And we need more of them.

You can build your lens. And of course, you could have built one yesterday, but you didn't. You didn't because it's too much of a hassle and because it wouldn't have been worth the trouble. It would be great if someone World make it easier.

So, Squidoo. Squidoo organizes lenses. We host them for free. We make them easy to build.

# Who needs to build a lens?

1. If you have a **blog**, a lens is a great way to highlight your best posts, to feature a commented version of your blogroll, and to point to the products and services that you write about, read about, enjoy, or want to see succeed. A lens will allow you and your blog to have a bigger share of the commentary and influence on your topic of choice.

2. If you have a **Web site** and you're not happy with your PageRank, a lens will increase it. That's because a lens provides exactly what search engines are looking for: authoritative insight so people can find what they're looking for. (That's why wikipedia ranks so highly on search engines— they provide a good experience and satisfied searchers are what search engines are seeking.)

3. If you have a **hobby**, creating a lens with tips and tools and examples and stuff is a faster and easier way to start than writing a blog about it. Once you've got a following, your blog will be a lot easier to dive into.

4. If you're a **newshound**, a lens allows you to highlight important mainstream and non-mainstream stories for your readers. And to do it in an easy-to-follow, non-time-based way. Yes, you can improve it every day if you want to, but no, you

don't have to keep pushing important parts of your archive off the page.

5. If you're a **fan**, a lens lets you share your take on the object of your affections—without the grind of a daily obligation to update.

6. If you're an **entrepreneur**, your lens on a popular topic could generate three or five or twenty dollars a day in clickthrough and affiliate income. Which doesn't sound like much, until you start thinking like an eBay PowerSeller and build twenty or even fifty lenses on a variety of topics. Did you know that 750,000 people make a full- or part-time living on eBay now? The same effect will probably happen with lenses. Don't quit your job yet, but if you build the right lenses and promote them, you ought to earn some royalties.

# Isn't a lens just a Web site?

A LENS IS A WEB SITE, but it's a very **specific** sort of Web site. It's a site with a defined layout and UI, and it is linked to millions of other lenses. Blogs are also just a Web site, but the easy interface and accepted conventions stand them apart. Same deal with lenses.

Because a lens can't do everything, you won't have to compete with those inclined to add bells and whistles and designs and sophisticated interfaces. Because a lens doesn't hold content (it just points to it), a lens will not replace the Web site you already have. Instead, a lens is a signpost, an organized pointer living in a site filled with other, similarly formatted pointers. Unlike a blog, a lens updates itself (if you want it to) with RSS feeds and Web services. This means that many lenses will do fine without a lot of tweaking and maintenance.

> The structured nature of Web 2.0, combined with the folksonomy of tags, makes a lens the perfect middleman between the content and expertise you've already got, and the surfers you've never met.

**EVERYONE'S AN EXPERT (ON SOMETHING)** Seth Godin

# When should you start?

SQUIDOO.COM KEEPS TRACK OF MILLIONS OF LENSES. We host them and know what is on each one. Each lens is scored by our proprietary LensRank algorithm, which ensures that the best lenses get the most traffic. And, like blogs, like everything in fact, there will probably be an A-list. How do you get on the A-list? Start early. Update often. Listen to your Web surfers—they can contact you directly from your lens. Build an audience. Link hither and yon and back again.

For old-timers, it's 1999 all over again. Some organizations decided to sit that fast-growth era out. It cost too much and was way too frothy. This time, though, it's a lot cheaper and a lot faster. Probably worth a try. After all, someone is going to build a lens about you and your area of expertise or passion. Might as well be you.

Squidoo.com is in a closed beta right now, at least until we get most of the bugs out. Visit us (http://www.squidoo.com), and we'll let you know as soon as we're ready to help you get started. In the meantime, start finding those links and focusing your lens.

Everyone's an expert (about something). What's your topic?

# EVERYONE'S AN EXPERT (ON SOMETHING) Seth Godin

# Ten examples of how to make Squidoo work for you

1. If I had a Web site that sold hospital cribs, I'd build a lens that taught people newly in the market for a hospital crib what they needed to know about this strange new world. I'd include links to my company and my competitors. I'd include links to support networks. I'd find services that help navigate the insurance maze. I'd put in a list of the top ten things to do before spending a penny.

2. If I were an author, I'd include links to all my books on Amazon, together with a pithy abstract on each one. I'd also include links to other authors who I thought were interesting. I'd have an automatically updated link that inserted my three most recent blog posts. I'd also include the RSS feed from a technorati search, showing surfers recent blogs that have mentioned me. I'd include links to conferences where I was speaking, and perhaps a top-ten list of the best ways to understand my writing. And I'd certainly have a box pointing to my best (and my worst) reviews.

3. If I were a religious evangelist, I'd have a lens that highlights my favorite Bible verses. The lens would use a Google map to give directions to my church and to other churches like mine. I'd include links to inspirational art and music and to the books that changed my life. I'd also have a big section devoted to my blog and to the blogs of my parishioners—updated automatically and delivering the three most recent posts from each. Finally, I'd include a module that links to several major online retailers so that my congregation could spend their money online while easily earning money for the church.

4. If I were a yo-yo expert, I'd have a lens that was nothing but links to tricks. I'd rank my favorite 100 tricks and point, one by one, to the best examples of those tricks on the Web. And maybe I'd point to Infinite Illusions, the online yo-yo store.

5. If I were an association chairman, I'd have a lens that pointed to my association's site and to members' sites.
I'd also feature a conference calendar from EVDB that would make it really clear to anyone in my industry which conferences were happening where. Even better, I'd challenge each and every one of our members to have a lens, too. Those lenses would help them professionally and, by pointing back to the association, would contribute to our position in the community. And better still, I'd have an RSS feed that would make it easy for every

single member to add my latest rants to their lenses.

6. If I were a podcaster, I'd definitely have a lens. It would list the details of my podcasts, point to transcripts that some fan had posted, point to my six most recent podcasts, and include the RSS for subscribing to the podcast. The lens would also have a set of links for finding out about podcasting and getting a podcast reader.

7. If I were a pharmacy in Canada, I'd have a lens that pointed to Better Business Bureau reports on overseas pharmacies, to online testimonials on people's blogs, and to my site. I'd also point to my competitors' sites to demonstrate how fairly I was treating my customers.

8. If I were the Juvenile Diabetes Research Foundation, I'd invite all 45,000 of my most important donors to build sites on their favorite topics. The invitation would set the default royalty cash flow to "Donate my royalties to JDRF." If each lens generated as little as $2 a day, that'd be a whole bunch of money earned for the charity. We'd also earn a bounty on every successful lensmaster we brought in.

9. If I were an eBay seller, I'd have a lens devoted to my auctions of gardening equipment. It would update automatically, of course, so I wouldn't even have to tweak it to keep it current. I'd surround the

listings with quotes from my happy customers and background information on my life as a gardener.

10. If I were Howard Dean, I'd have 50,000 active Democrats each build a lens with his or her particular take on politics. I'd let these people know that they could easily include an RSS feed that would allow me (Howard) to insert today's talking point automatically on their lenses every day.

11. (A bonus.) If I were a person (and I am), I'd have a lens about... me. A lens that listed my blog and my recent posts and my bio and my work history and my Amazon wish list and my Flickr account and whatever I wanted the public to know about me. Because sooner or later, the public *is* going to know about me, so I might as well tell them the story I want them to hear. Would you hire someone if she didn't have a lens?

# Take a look at some great lenses (these go live October 18th, 2005)

If you'd like to see a lens...

... that a jobseeker might build, visit
http://www.squidoo.com/samples/jobs.

... that a radio station might build, visit
http://www.squidoo.com/samples/radio.

... that an entrepreneur seeking income might
build, visit
http://www.squidoo.com/samples/royalties.

... that a celebrity might build, visit
http://www.squidoo.com/samples/oprah.

... that a political activist might build, visit
http://www.squidoo.com/samples/rwanda.

... that a fan might build, visit
http://www.squidoo.com/samples/GoYanks

... that an author might build, visit
http://www.squidoo.com/samples/sethgodin

Every lens has a unique name—a URL within Squidoo that's like a domain. Once it's taken, it's gone. Sign up for our private beta so you can grab the name you want:
http://www.squidoo.com/secretbeta.

Step 1: Focus
Step 2: Make it clear
Step 3: Build your lenses
Step 4: Link to the blogosphere
Step 5: Repeat

See you there.

# ABOUT THE AUTHOR:

Seth Godin is the author of seven books that have been bestsellers around
the world. His last book was written with 32 other authors, and all royalties go straight to charity.

Nearly ten years ago, Seth founded Yoyodyne, which originated the idea of permission marketing online. After Yoyodyne was acquired by Yahoo, he served as VP Direct Marketing for Yahoo for about a year. In 2000, Godin focused full-time on his career as an acclaimed public speaker, an author and a blogger. Seven of Seth's books have been bestsellers somewhere around the world, and his blog has been picked as the best business blog by several leading publications including *Forbes, Marketing Sherpa* and *ClickZ.*
Godin is the founder of Squidoo.com.

# BN Publishing
# We have Book Recommendations for you

*Automatic Wealth: The Secrets of the Millionaire Mind--Including: Acres of Diamonds, As a Man Thinketh, I Dare you!, The Science of Getting Rich, The Way to Wealth, and Think and Grow Rich*
by Napoleon Hill, et al

*Think and Grow Rich [MP3 AUDIO] [UNABRIDGED]*
by Napoleon Hill, Jason McCoy (Narrator)

*As a Man Thinketh [UNABRIDGED]*
by James Allen, Jason McCoy (Narrator)

*Your Invisible Power: How to Attain Your Desires by Letting Your Subconscious Mind Work for You [MP3 AUDIO] [UNABRIDGED]*
by Genevieve Behrend, Jason McCoy (Narrator)

*Thought Vibration or the Law of Attraction in the Thought World [MP3 AUDIO] [UNABRIDGED]*
by William Walker Atkinson, Jason McCoy (Narrator)

www.ingramcontent.com/pod-product-compliance
Lightning Source LLC
LaVergne TN
LVHW042351060326
832902LV00006B/538